Drawing Steampunk

By Amy Hughes

Table of Contents

Chapter 1 – Where did Steampunk come from?

Most people think this genre was born in the 1980's, but in actuality, it has been living in books since the 19th century. Novels like *Frankenstein* and *Twenty Thousand Leagues Under the Sea* gave us a glimpse of Victorian style mixed with industrial accents. Even *The Time Machine* had Steampunk style in the way Wells described the machine itself. It started gaining steam in the 70's, and really came into its own in the 80's.

Hollywood's love for the genre has been seen in movies like *Van Helsing, The League of Extraordinary Gentlemen,* both *Sherlock Holmes* films which starred Robert Downey Jr. and many more. There are even Steampunk elements in animated films by Hayao Myazaki.

It combines elements of Victorian style and architecture and steam powered industrial machines. Every bit of Steampunk has mechanical and personal touches. You notice gear work, steam pipes, and other industrial accents. They comfortably blend both style, form, and function. You will find out how to incorporate all those elements in each art piece you draw.

Chapter 2 – What do I need to get started?

Every craft or art has its own set of equipment, and drawing is no different. You don't need top-of-the-line tools to start, but you do need a few things:

• Pencils, a good set of art pencils with different leads is important. The harder the lead, the more it can help you start the sketch. The softer the lead, the easier it is to add shadows and shading.

• Sketch paper, this tends to come in the form of a pad, and these pads come in different sizes. A standard size of 9" by 12" should give you the size you need to layout your sketch and fill it in without you having to worry about running out of paper space.

• Compasses/templates, these may sound weird in relation to drawing, but Steampunk does incorporate a lot of circles and circular designs. Your craft store should have a compass or sets of circle templates. These will come in handy.

• Erasers, you will need a couple of different ones. A kneading eraser can help smudge places in your shading to create the illusion of where the light hits the object. A standard rubber eraser will also come in handy to get rid of rogue marks and preliminary sketch strokes.

• Smudge sticks, also known as stumps, are tightly rolled pieces of paper that are often sold in packs. These will help soften edges and smudge darkened areas where shadows and shading are needed.

• Eraser guard, this is a thin piece of metal that contains different holes in it. It works wonders for helping you erase just what you want gone.

• Dry erase bag is usually a white bag filled with eraser particles. This can be sprinkled over a finished piece and the particles rubbed to remove rogue smudges from where you hand may have lain on the drawing and then somewhere else on the paper.

• A comfortable workspace, this is a must for your back. Your space must promote good posture and be comfortable enough for you to work without having to shift to get into a better position.

• Models/references, even though we provide you with a start in this book, you will probably want to further your drawing skills. Every artist uses references to draw from. This can be anything from pictures on the internet to pictures of everyday household objects and even your family.

A short note on lead...

HB Graphite Scale

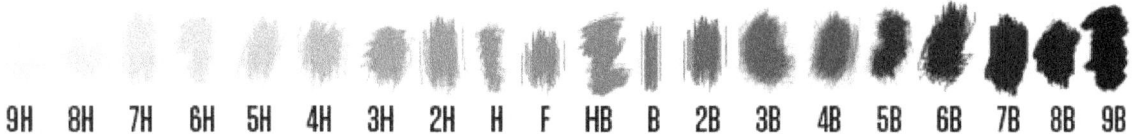

| 9H | 8H | 7H | 6H | 5H | 4H | 3H | 2H | H | F | HB | B | 2B | 3B | 4B | 5B | 6B | 7B | 8B | 9B |

I have included this guide on the different leads that are used in drawing and shading. The softer leads provide darker shading, and the harder leads barely leave a pencil mark. Many artists use the harder ones to layout their work.

Chapter 3 – Just a few reminders

I know you're ready to jump in a get ready, but there are a few things you need to keep in mind before you get started with your first lesson.

• **You're getting started.** Don't expect to be perfect from the first pencil stroke. Take your time, and you'll get it. Your first projects can take as long as a few hours.

• **You can only improve you.** Learning something new is not a race. Don't worry about how good others are doing. It's easy to look online and see all the elaborate drawings and get discouraged when yours doesn't seem to match up. Keep in mind they too started somewhere and their pieces were not perfect either. Every once in a while, go back to your previous work and compare it to what you have done recently. This will show you how far you've come.

• **If you need to repeat a lesson, go for it.** If you feel you are not ready to progress to another lesson in this book, stay where you are at until you are comfortable. Work at your own pace. Repeat lessons as many times as you see fit.

• **Keep it simple.** We will start out with simple sketches and move onto more and more difficult pieces. We will break it down step-by-step to make it easier for you to follow.

• **Do your own thing.** Practice makes perfect. Do be afraid snap pictures of nature, buildings, and all sorts of other things to add a Steampunk flair. Try different things. Draw different objects. Don't limit yourself to just one aspect of Steampunk. After all it's an entire world.

Chapter 4 – Dancing Couple

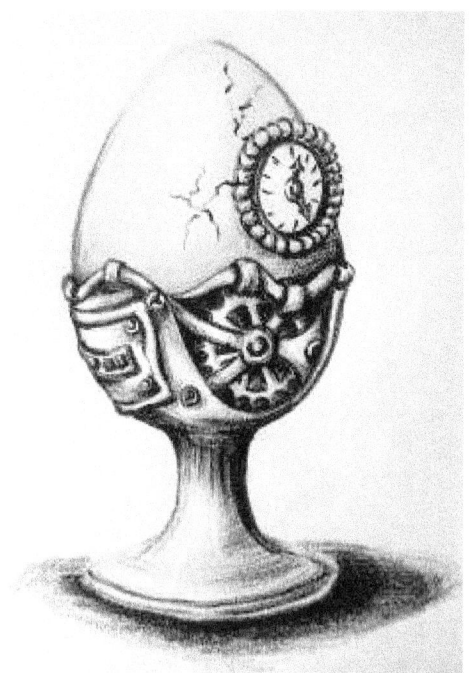

Most of us have heard of Faberge and his famous jeweled eggs. You can do the same when learning how to draw Steampunk. In this picture, you have a boiled egg in its stand and accent it with a watch face, and gear and we've even added metal plate.

The curves and simple form of the egg will be the first lesson in this book.

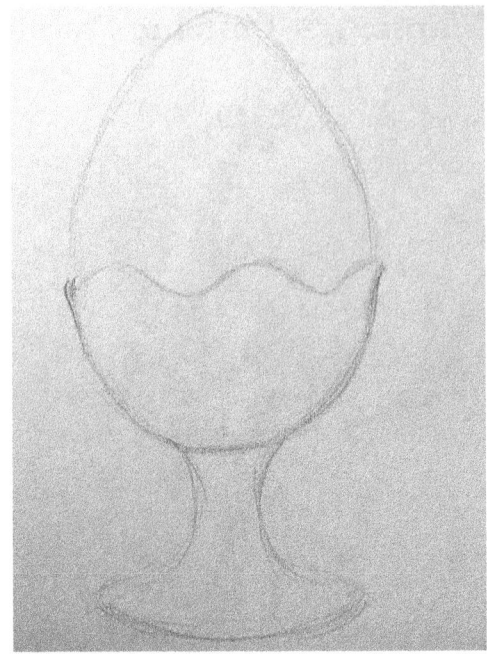

The best way to start this lesson is by drawing the whole egg first. Use the bottom of the egg to form the cup of the stand.

1. Draw a wave across the egg as you seen in the picture.

2. Draw facing curves coming down from the cup.

3. Draw an ellipse for the base.

4. Draw two circles in the upper right of the egg. This is the start of the watch face.

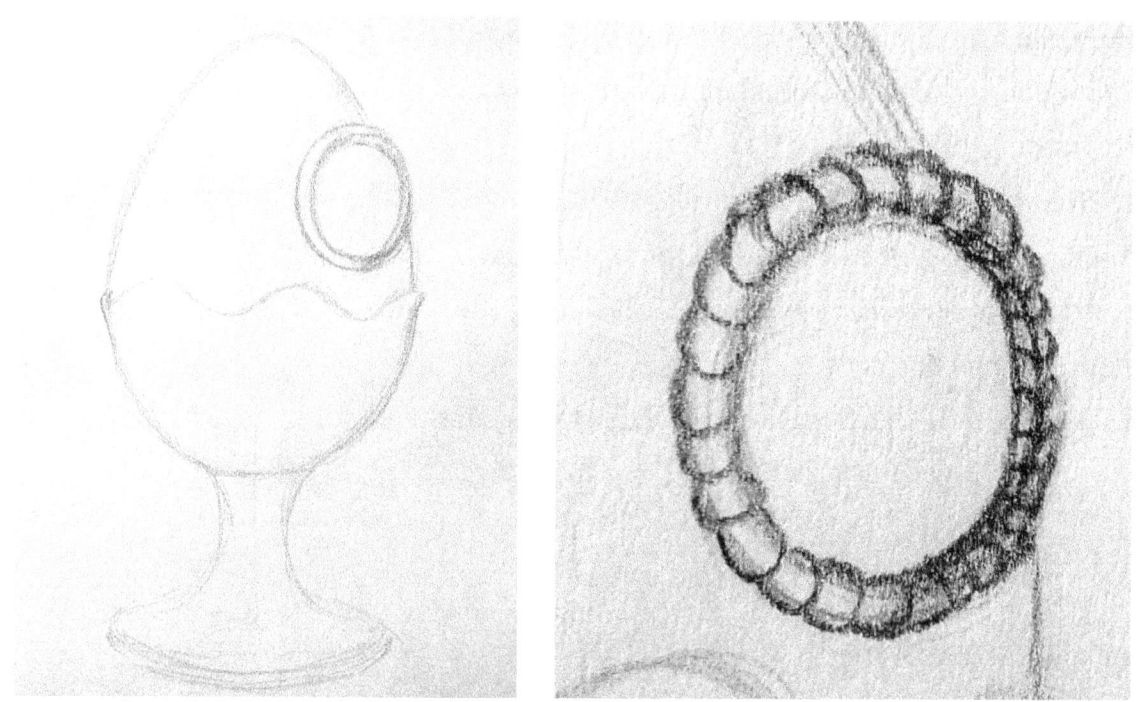

Here we are focusing on the watch face a little more. The coils are drawn by creating small curves around both circles. We are also drawing smaller lines on the inside to give it depth.

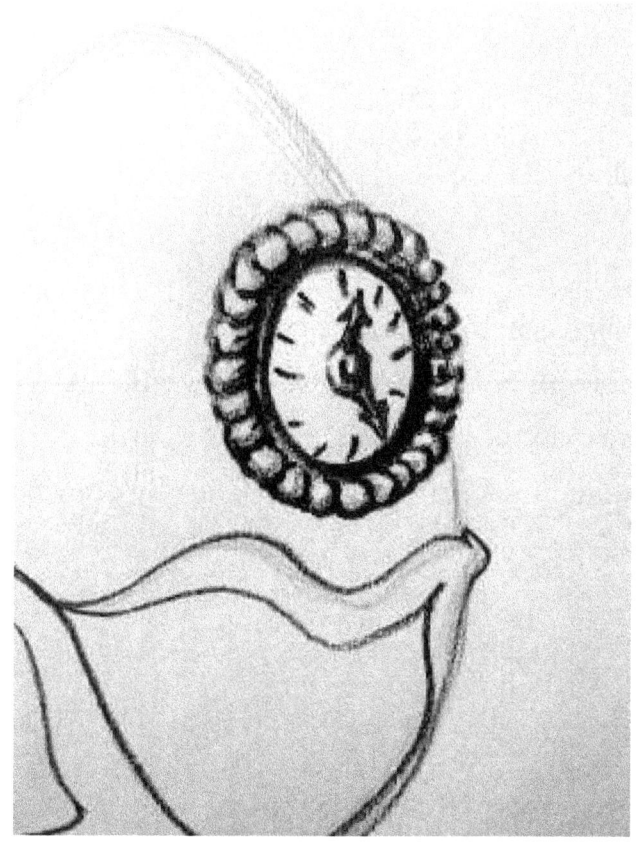

Here, we are adding in hash marks for the numbers. As this is a small detail in the watch, adding in actual numbers or Roman numerals would make it too crowded.

5. Draw two more circles in the watch.

6. Draw arrows for the hour and minute hands.

7. Add in a darker line around the inside of the watch to make the details in it stand out more.

8. Darken in the portion of the egg cup you see in the picture.

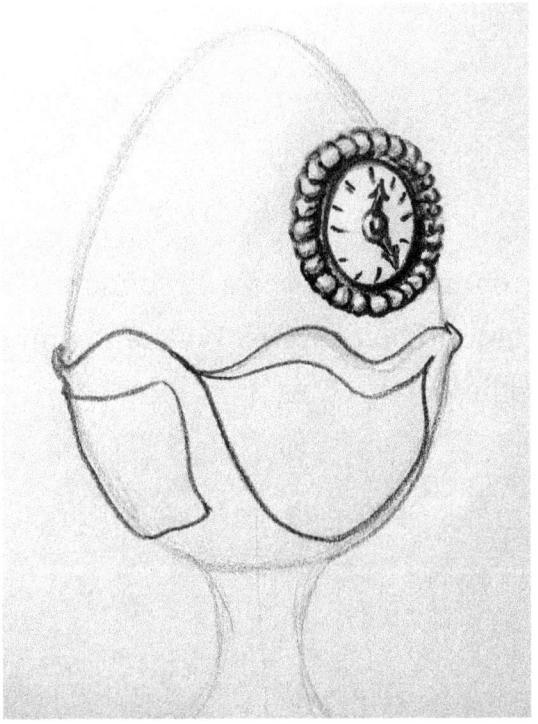

9. Add a little detailing as in the picture as well.

10. Zooming out now. As you can see, we have darkened in and adding more detailing to the egg cup in the next step.

11. In the most prominent part of the egg cup, start by drawing the circles for the gears.

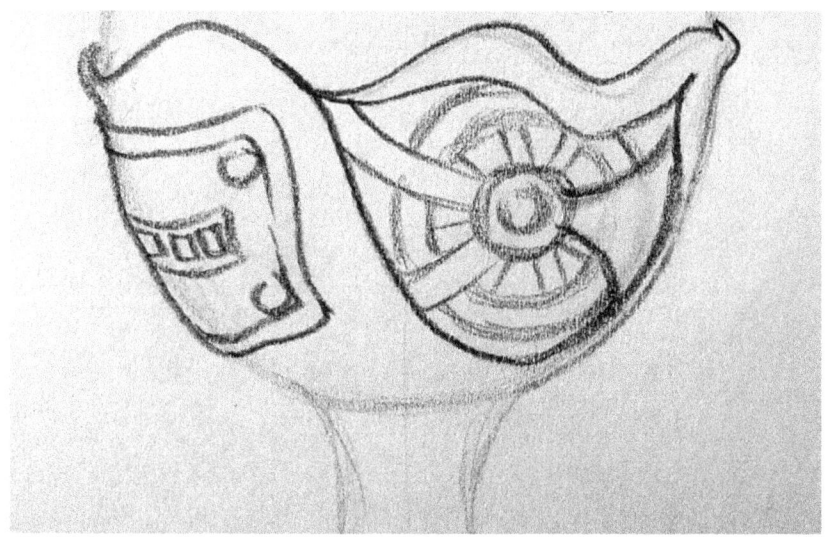

12. Draw the circles for the center of the section.

13. Draw the spokes as you see in the picture.

14. Draw the curves starting from the center circles to the edges.

15. Draw two curves on the right side starting from the center and going to the right edge.

16. On the left, start with a loose rectangle and circles for the rivets.

Draw an inner rectangle and add squares.

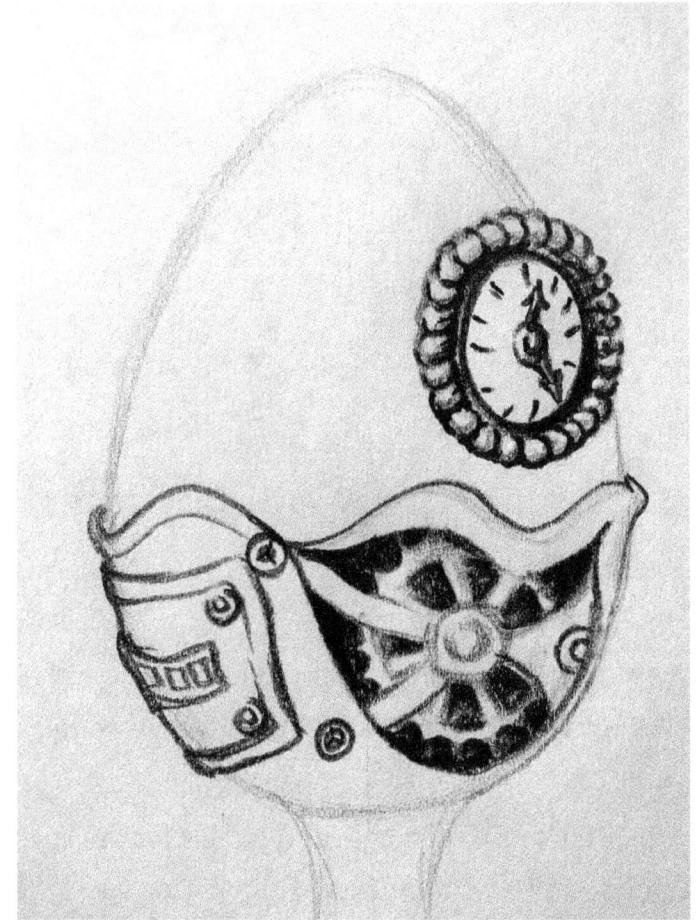

17. Shade in the parts around the gear.

18. Add in two small half-circles on the right side.

19. Add two screw heads on the left side between the two sections.

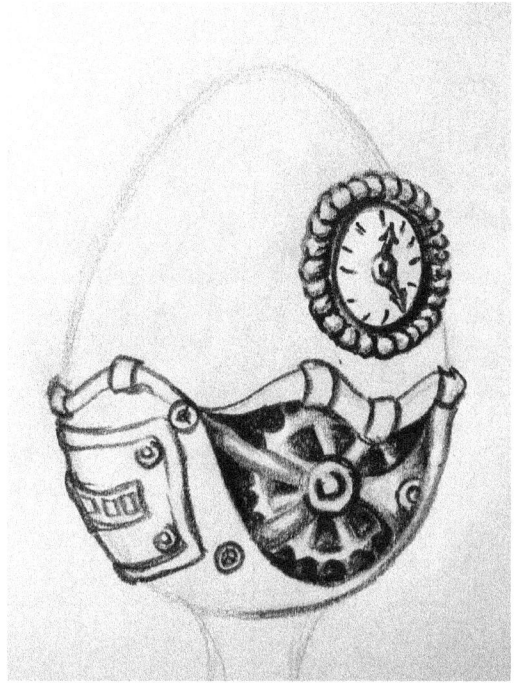

We're focusing on the curves on the edge of the cup.

20. Draw curves as you see in the picture for metal plating.

21. Go back to the gear on the bottom.

22. Using a softer lead, shade around the edges of the bands.

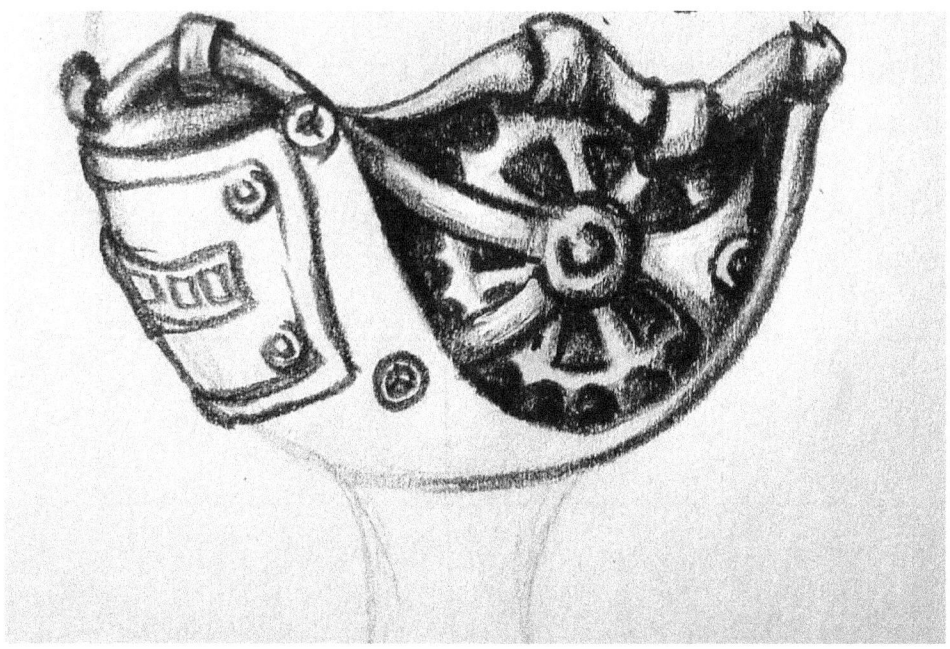

23. To shade as you see here, simply darken in the area just above the rectangle plate.

24. Darken the right of the cup.

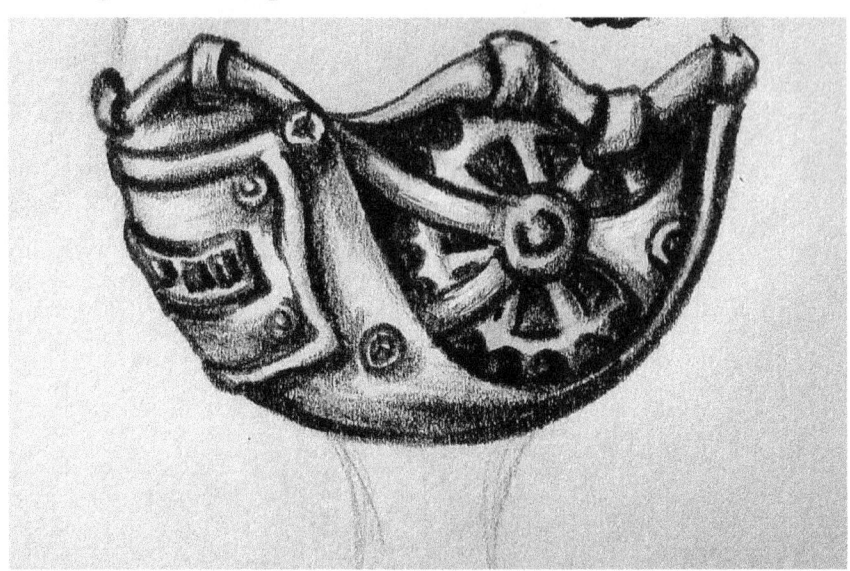

25. Darken the rest of the cup.

26. Now shade in as you see above. You can use a blending stump to shade more accurately.

We will now shade in the base of the cup.

27. Use short, light strokes at first, darkening it by going back over the original strokes.

28. To give the base a rounder feels, use a harder lead (2H) and make curved marks around the bottom.

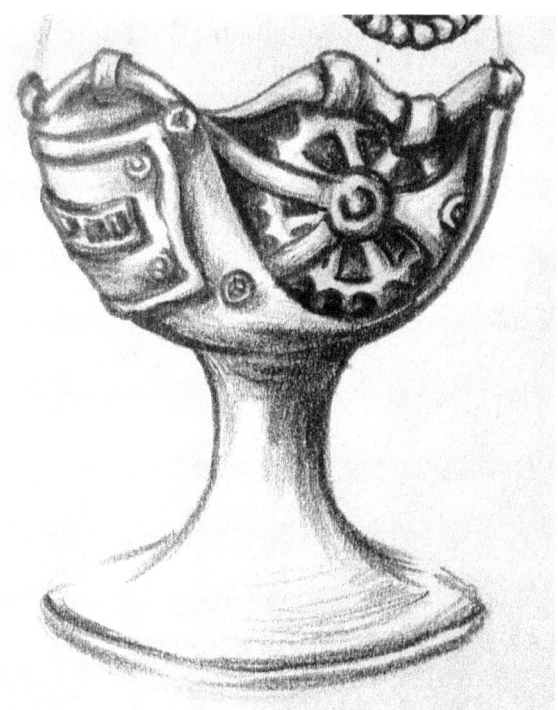

29. Darken in the rest of the lines for the base.

30. Here we add cracks to the egg, because, well, you can't just put a watch face on an egg without it breaking a bit, right?

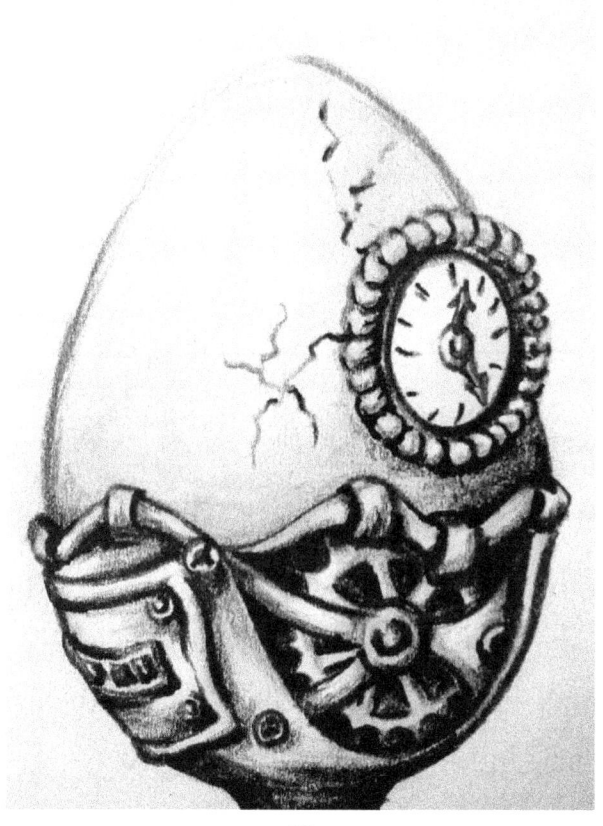

31. Add a little shading between the watch and the cup rim.

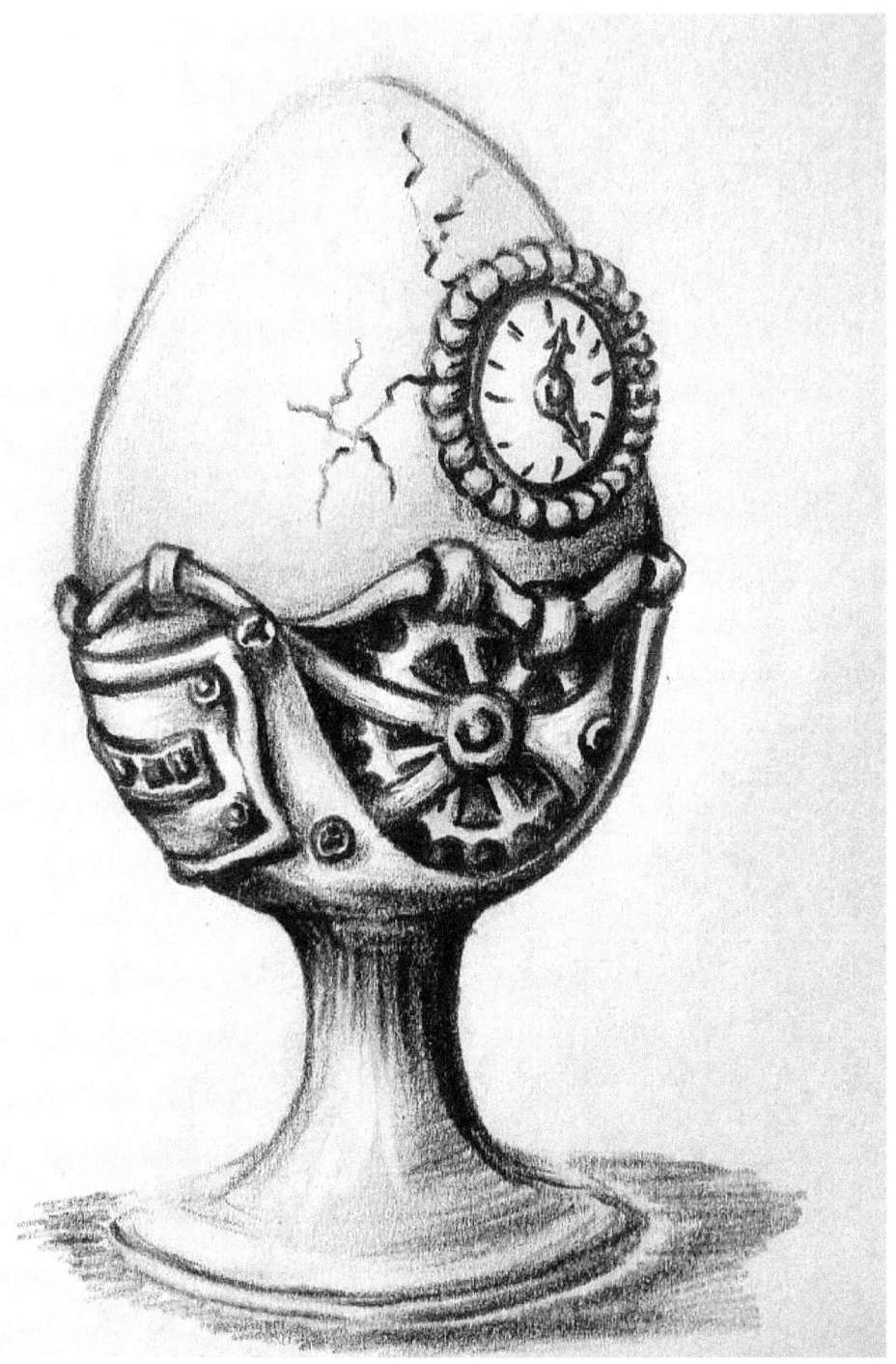

32. Add some shading to the far left as well.

33. We just need to add some more shading to the base and the area around the base as well. Everything leaves a shadow depending on the light source.

Can you tell where the light is coming from?

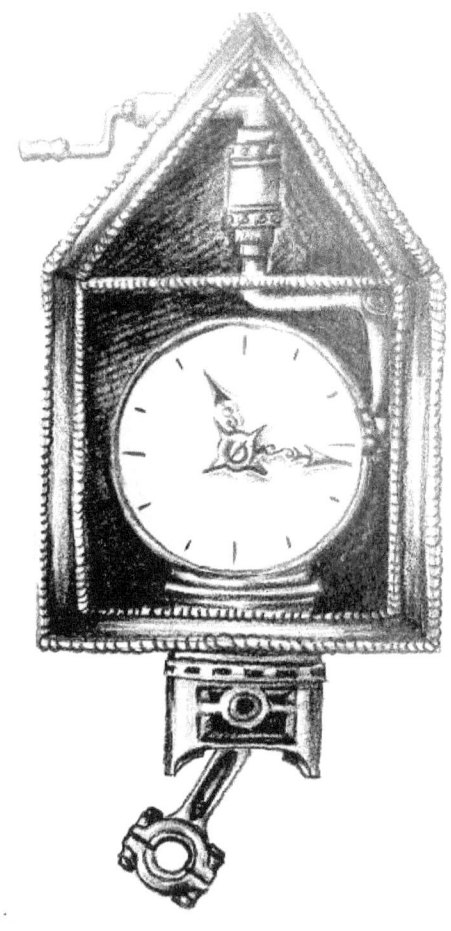

A simple time piece, when done in the Steampunk style, can be a thing of wonder. There is not limit as to how you can embellish it. It's up to you, ultimately. We're going to draw the simple style you see to the left.

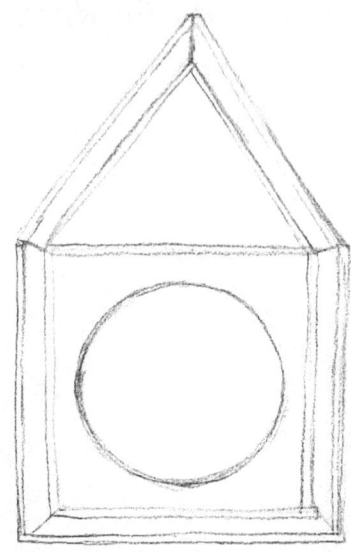

1. Start by drawing the circle in the center. This will help you frame it when you add the rest of the shapes.

2. Draw the squares around the circle.

3. Link them as you see in the picture.

4. Draw the triangles. If you want to center them a little more, draw a straight line through the center of the square, and then draw your lines to form the triangles.

5. Draw a small curve to the right of the circle, and then connect them using lines.

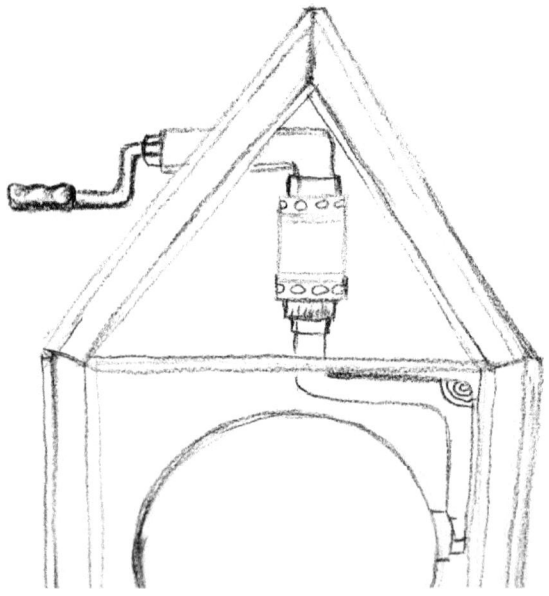

6. Draw curves going up and through to the top of the clock.

7. Draw small circles on the bend to the right on the piping.

8. For the tube in the triangle, start by drawing simple lines spaced apart like in the picture.

9. Connect them with two long lines.

10. Draw hash marks on the lower one.

11. Going up from there, add the ellipses going up the tube.

12. Draw an elbow bend leading out of the clock.

13. Draw a rounded rectangle with hash marks.

14. Now, draw a bent handle.

15. To make handle, draw a rounded rectangle first, and then add the bumps for the hand grips.

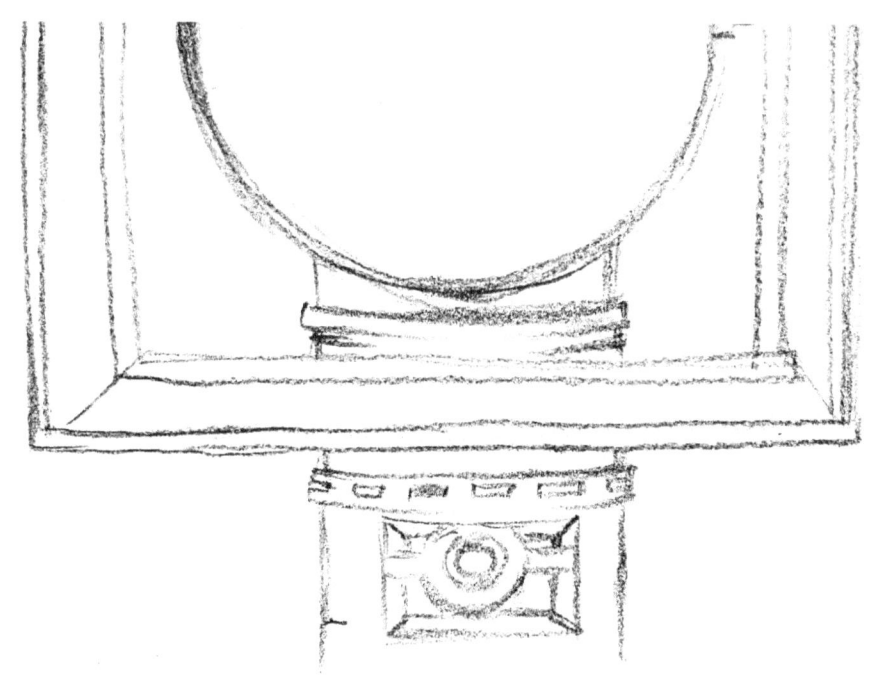

16. Under the main part of the clock, draw the beginnings of rectangle.

17. Draw a thin rectangle about a quarter of an inch down from the clock.

18. Draw smaller rectangles inside the thin triangle as you see in the picture.

19. Inside the main rectangle, draw a smaller one.

20. Now, draw a series of circles as you see in the picture.

21. Connect the outermost circle to the edges.

22. Now draw an even smaller rectangle in the inside and connect it to the one framing the circles via lines.

a. Draw the tube that is under the clock face in the picture;

b. Start with a simple rectangle.

c. Draw another, thinner one on top of the first.

d. Draw hash marks on either side of the rectangle as you see in the picture.

23. Make an ellipse under the rectangle you started in the previous picture.

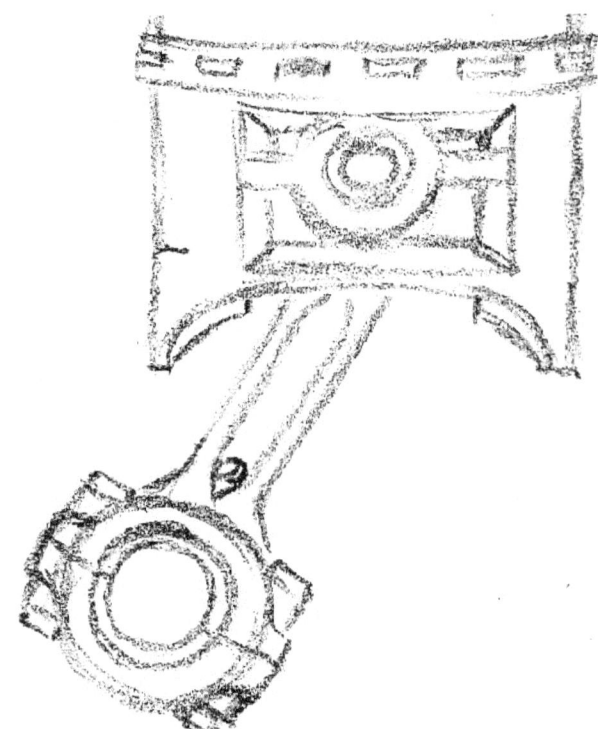

24. Add the smaller details like in the picture.

25. Start the pendulum by drawing lines down from the bottom of clock.

26. Draw a circle coming from the lines you have drawn.

27. Draw another circle outside the first.

28. Give it about a quarter of an inch, and draw a third.

29. Now, draw the squares you see on either side of the circles.

30. Connect the lines to the circles as in the picture.

31. Draw lines connecting the circles as in the picture.

32. Draw an arrow point above the circle.

33. Draw lines coming from it.

34. Finish off the detailing as you see in the picture.

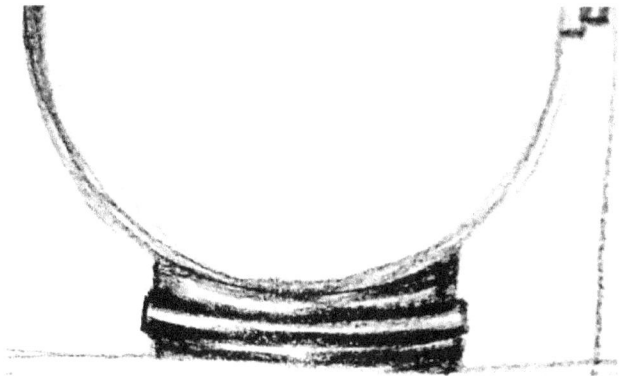

35. Shade in the tubing under the clock face as you see here. Use a soft lead. If you don't have one as soft as the diagram, repeatedly go over the shaded area until you get the shading you need.

36. In the next picture, we have shaded in the crack mechanism of the clock. Notice how we only shaded in one half of the tubing? This is because we are showing where the light is hitting the object.

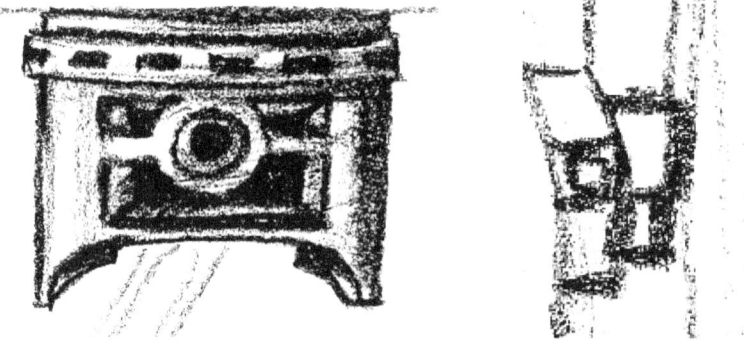

37. We have darkened in the small mechanisms to the right of the clock face.

38. Fill in the small rectangles in the piece below the clock face.

39. Fill in the space behind the circle below that.

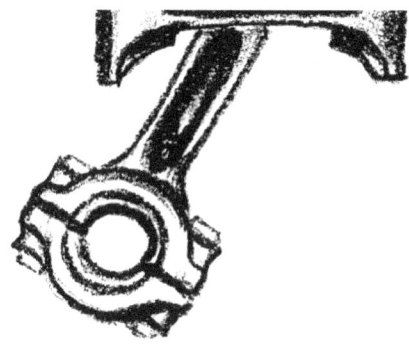

40. Shade the part as shown in the picture.

41. Darken the lines on the pendulum a shade as in the picture.

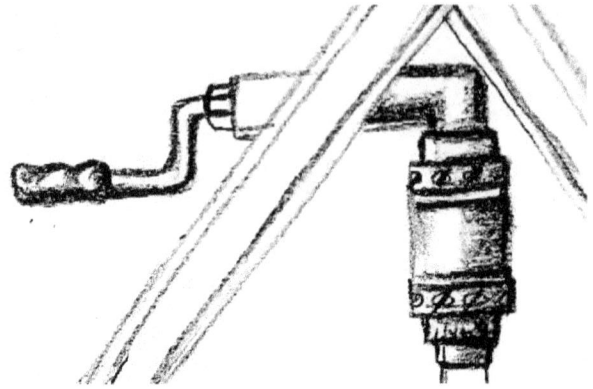

We are now focusing on the clock face.

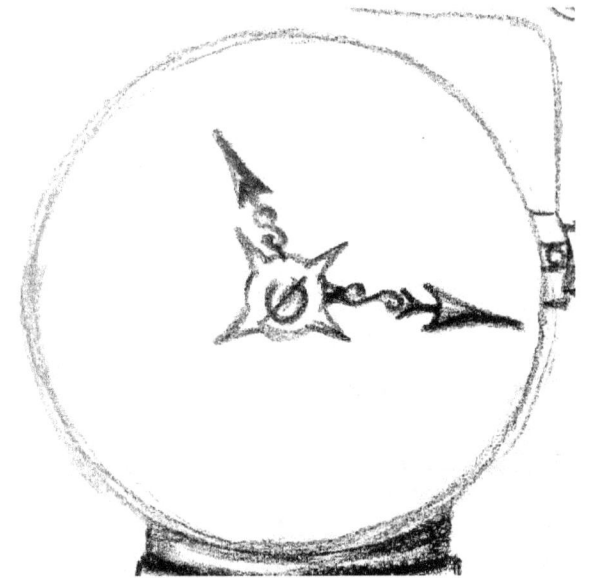

42. Draw an open circle in the middle.

43. Draw a light circle around the open one.

44. Add the points you see in the picture.

45. Erase the lines you don't need.

46. Draw a line through the center.

47. Draw very short lines to begin the hands.

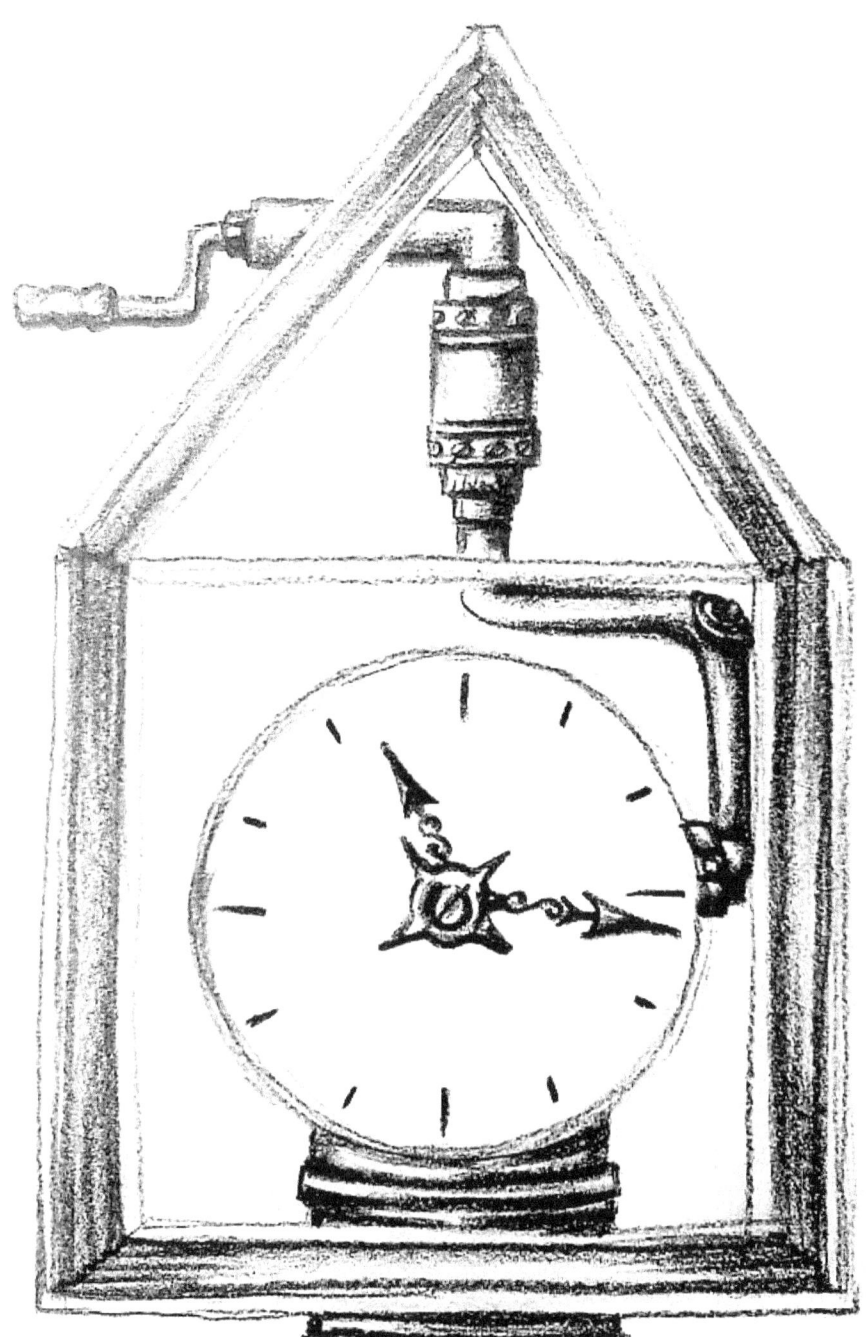

48. Make fancy "S" for the arms.

49. Draw the arrow heads as you see in the picture.

50. Shade as in the picture.

51. Shade the tubing to the right of the clock face.

52. Add the marks to represent the numbers on the clock face.

53. Shade in the center of the clock face as you see in the picture.

54. Darken in the top part where the tubing is.

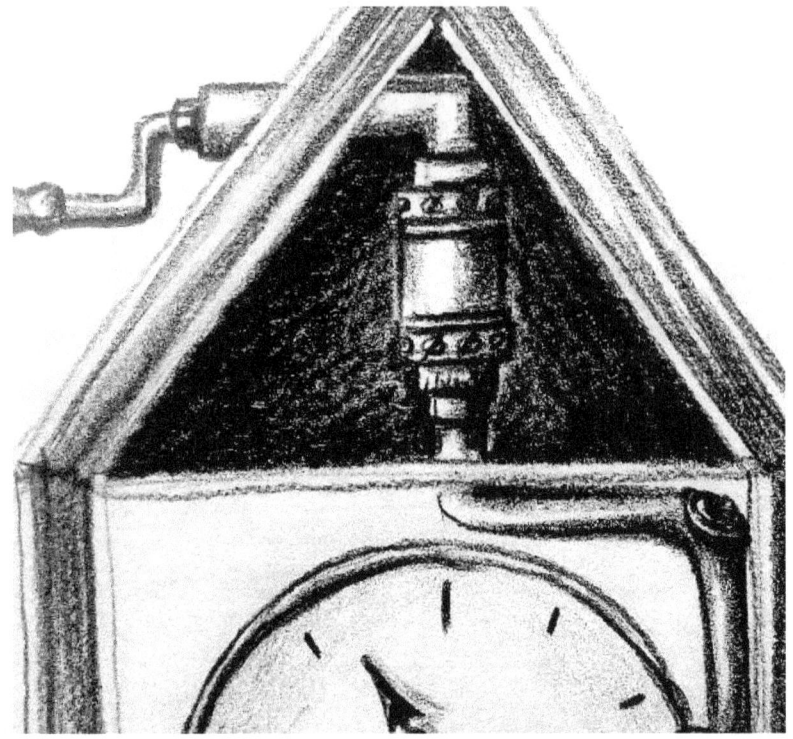

Look at the finished picture below.

55. We've added small lines each of the lines that are close together. This gives it texture and a feel of carved wood.

56. We've also shaded in the edge of the clock face.

57. Add shadows under the middle of the clock face and under the clock hands.

58. Darken in the area around the clock face.

59. Shade the areas around the frame as they are in the picture. Again, there are light and dark spots according to how the light hits the clock. You can use you smudge stick to blend the shadows.

Can you see anything else we did in the picture?

Chapter 6 - A Child's Toy

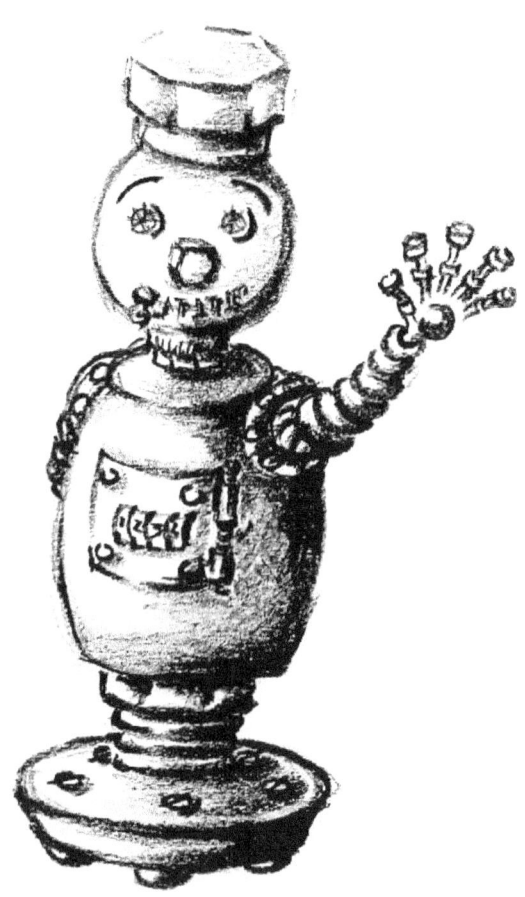

From water guns to computers, there is no limit to what you can embellish in the Steampunk style. To the left, we have a simple child's toy. He looks cheerful with his smile, and he is also waving at us. Let's get started…

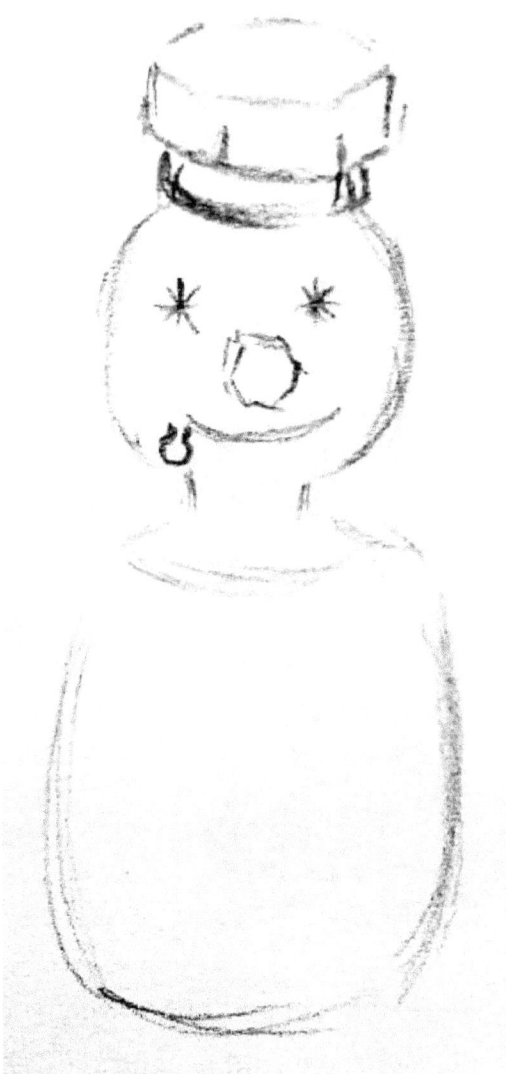

1. Start out drawing the body, which is a rectangle with rounded corners.

2. The top of the rectangle is a circle.

3. Draw two short lines for the neck.

4. Draw a rounded square for the head.

5. A curved rectangle is on top of the head.

6. About a quarter inch above the rounded rectangle, draw the hexagon you see in the picture.

7. Roughly sketch the front of the hat below the hexagon.

8. Draw light hash marks to finish the hat.

9. Draw asterisks for the eyes.

10. We have another bolt for the nose.

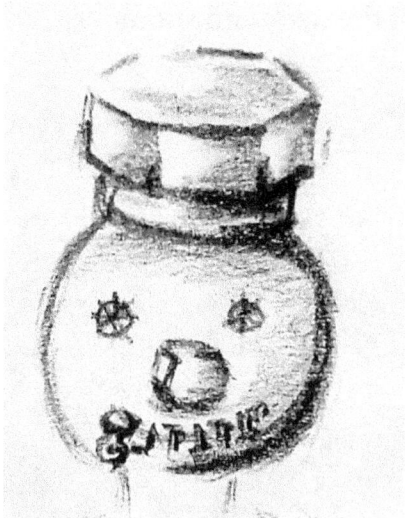

Draw a smile on our little guy and the pipe you see in the picture. I have zoomed in on the head. Add hash marks to the mouth.

1. Draw circles around the eyes.

2. Lightly shade in the face and hat. Take note of where the light is hitting the face.

3. Don't forget to darken the lines on the head and hat.

4. To focus on the neck, darken the lines.

5. Add a tapered tube under the main one as in the picture.

6. Add hash marks and the thick part of the neck

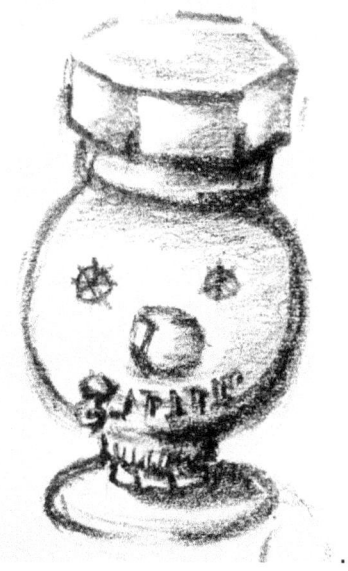

7. Make separate rectangles for the tapered part of the neck.

8. Shade in the right side of the neck and shoulder.

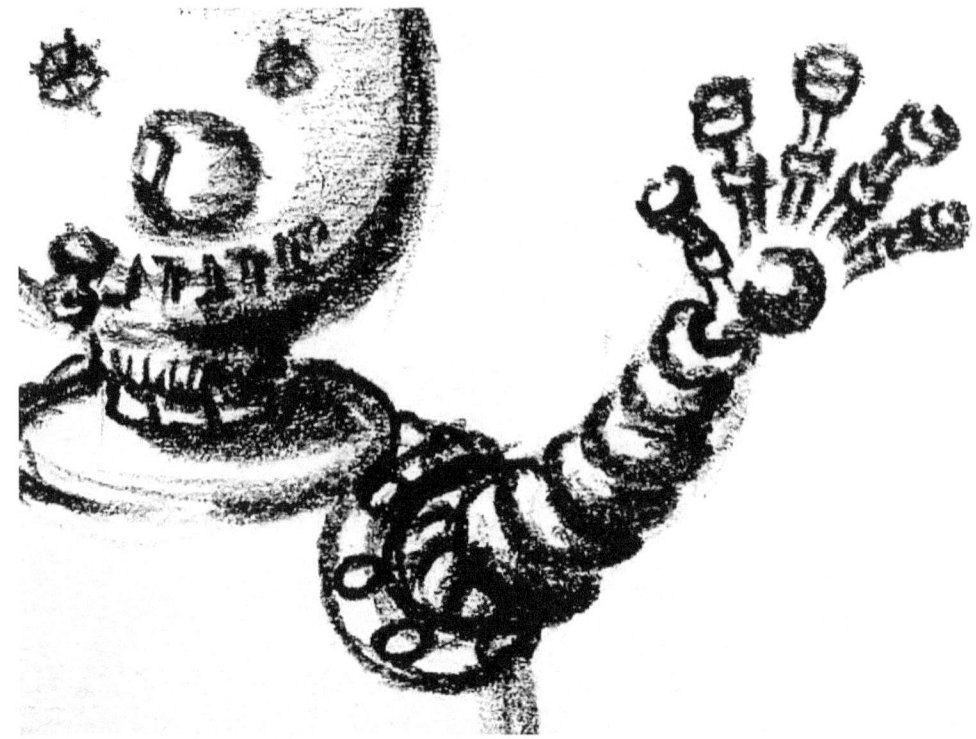

9. Staring from the left, make a curve.

10. Fill it in with small circles.

11. On the right, make a series of circles for the shoulder socket and the arms.

12. Draw small circles around the main part.

13. Make hash marks to the right of the circles.

14. Make light marks for the fingers.

15. Darken all the lines.

16. Draw a circle and shade all but the small portion you see in the picture for the palm.

17. Draw the nuts for fingers. Draw small pipes to connect the nuts.

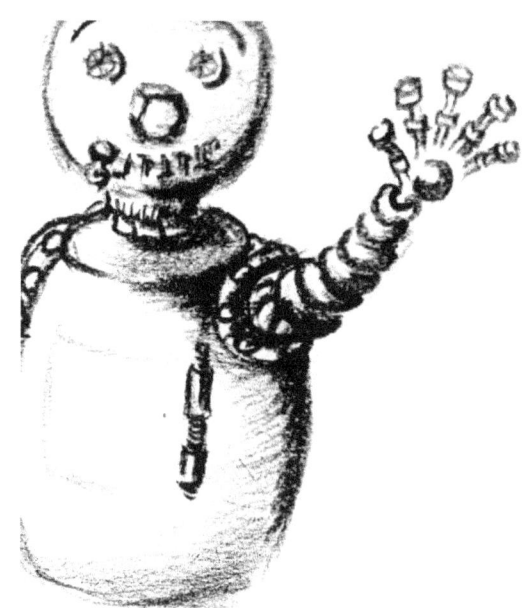

18. Connect it to the arm.

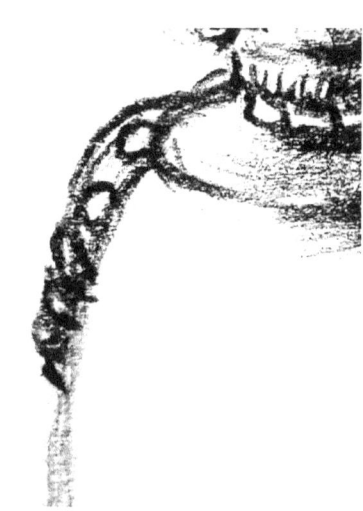

19. Shade the bottom of the arm, and smudge to soften the shading.

20. For the left arm, draw the same bumps you did for the right hand. This will give the hint there are two arms and not one.

21. Shade in the right side as you see in the picture.

22. Use the smudge stick to soften the shading.

23. Now, draw two rectangles and a few bumps for screw grooves.

24. Draw an outline of a rectangle. Don't darken it in yet.

25. Darken the lines of the screws and hinges.

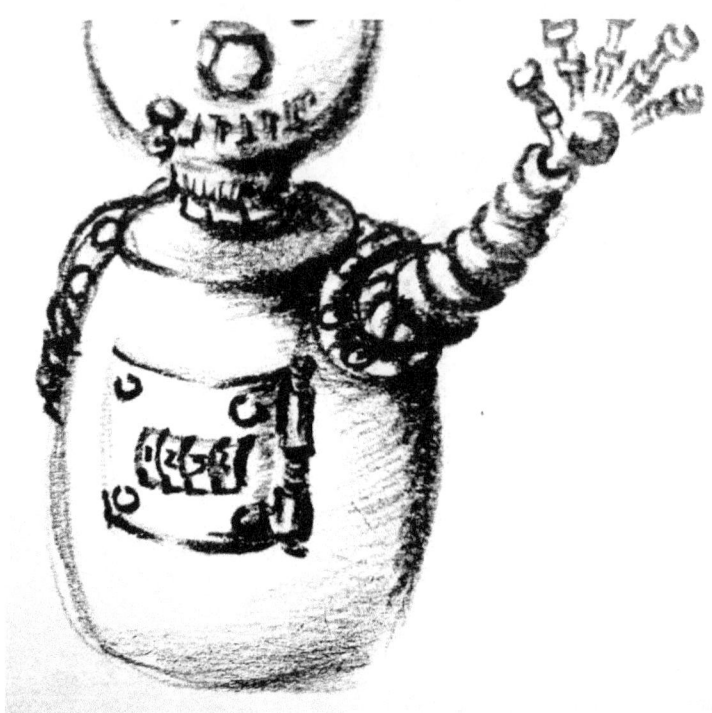

26. Make darker lines for the top and bottom of the plate.

27. Make circles for screws on each corner.

28. Draw bumps in the middle of the plate.

29. Lightly connect them all.

30. Add the numbers you see in the picture.

31. Add the shading you see in the picture.

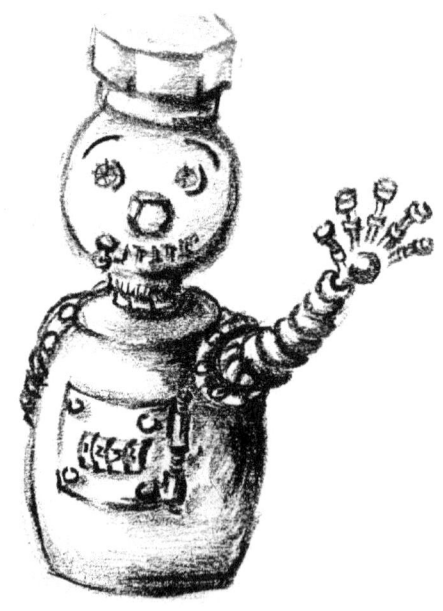

32. Keep in mind the light source.

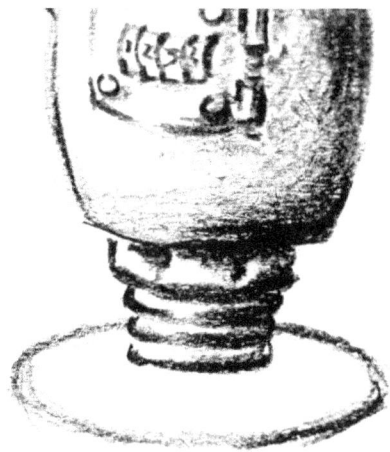

33. Make rounded rectangles, like the ones in the picture.

34. Don't forget to taper them as you go down to the base.

35. Hint at bolts by using shading.

36. Draw an ellipse for the base.

37. Draw the screws you see in the picture.

38. Shade as you see in the picture.

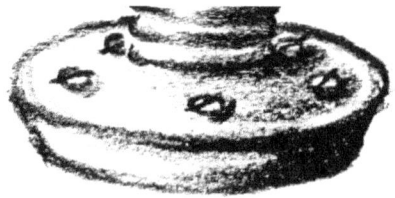

39. Taper the next layer.

40. Draw a curve to finish off the lower layer.

41. Shade as you see in the picture.

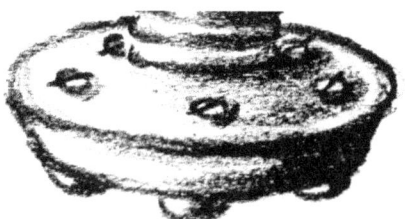

Draw the bumps for the bottom of the base.

42. Shade as in the picture.

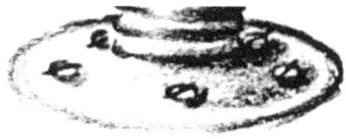

Chapter 7 - One cool cat...

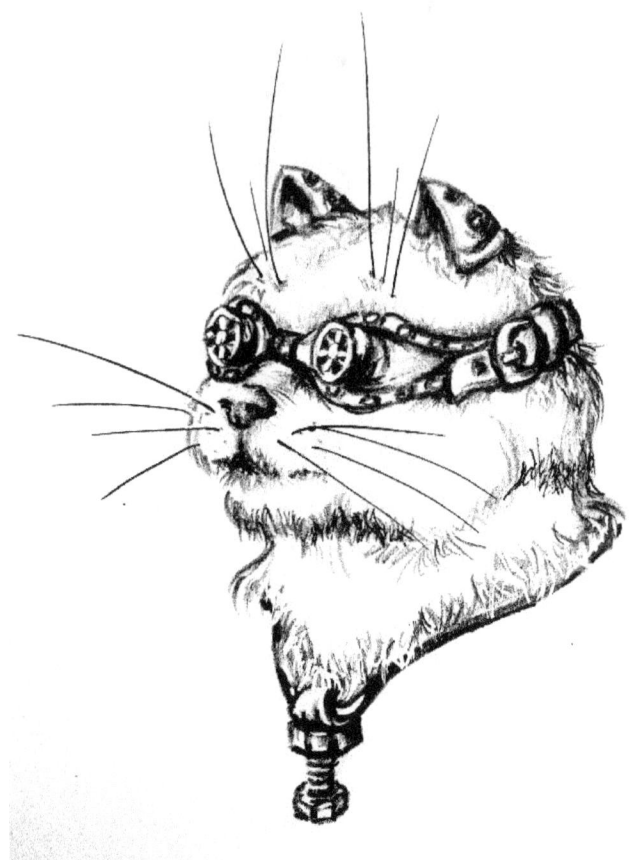

Another endearing quality of Steampunk is the wonderful way it gives animals human qualities. They make dogs and cats walk on two legs, and can even make a turtle sport a small radar dish.

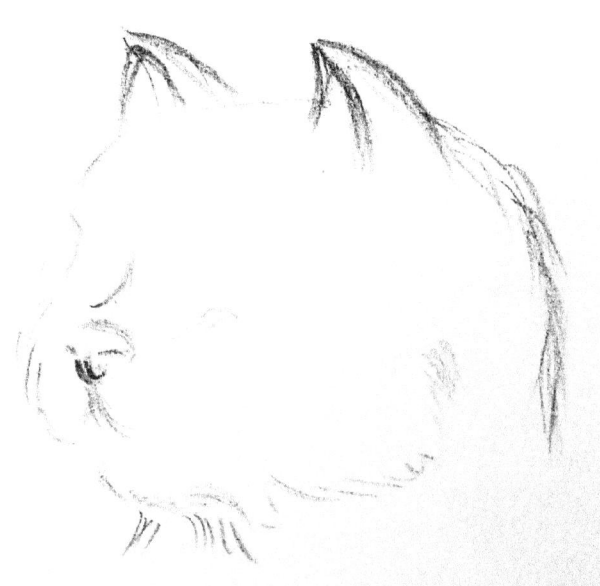

In this picture, we've given out feline friend, metal ears, goggles and even a collar with a pendant. In this picture, it is best to draw curves where the fur is to get a better idea of where to put the fur.

1. Draw the nose.
2. Use triangles for the ears. Round them off when you are finished.
3. Fill in the lines with fur.

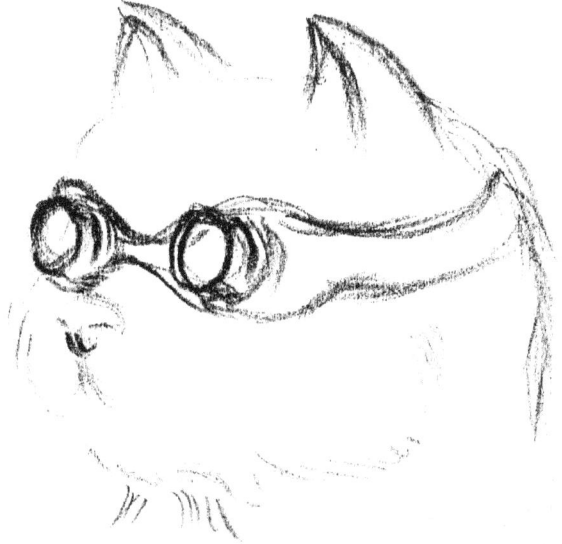

4. Draw curves from the back of the head and around to the front.
5. Draw two more curves where the frames are going to go.

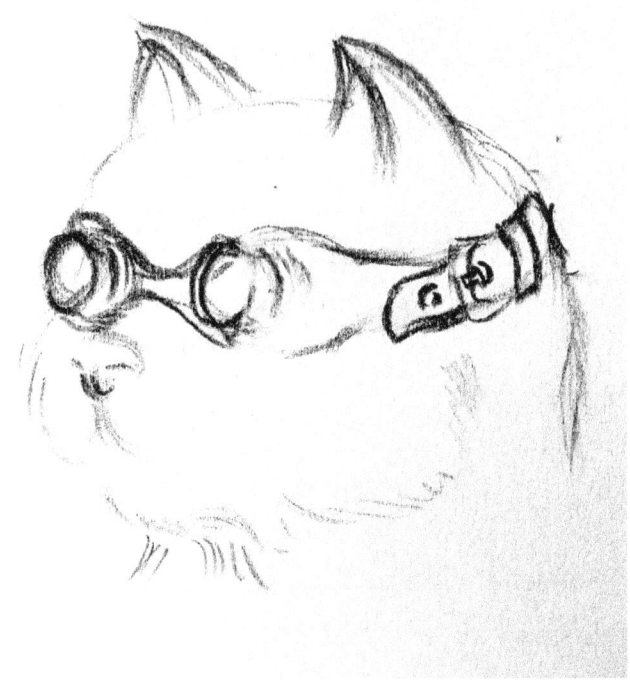

6. Draw the frames using circles and more curves. Don't worry about it being a little rough at first.

7. Darken in the back side of the headband.

8. Draw curves for the strap catch.

9. Draw two rounded squares for the buckle.

10. Draw two curves for the bump the latch creates in the belt.

11. Taper off the belt draw a curve and connect it back to where the buckle is.

12. Draw a circle for last hole in the headband strap.

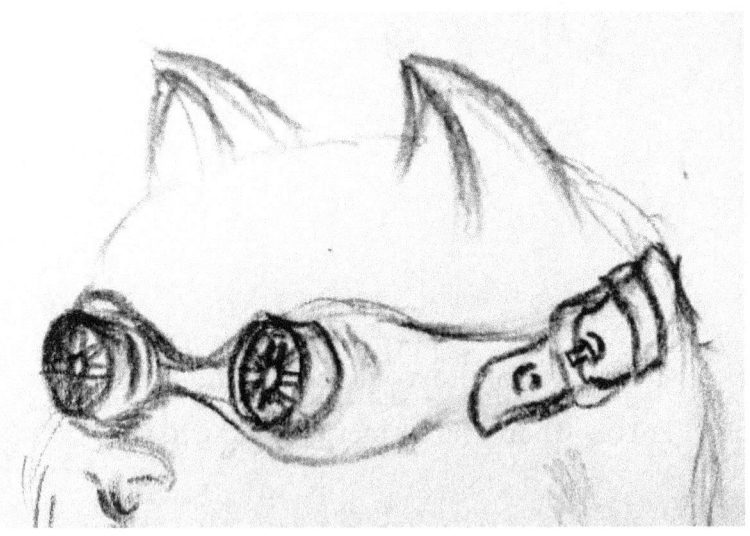

13. Darken the circles you made earlier.

14. Draw a smaller circle in the of the bigger ones.

15. Draw spokes coming out from the center.

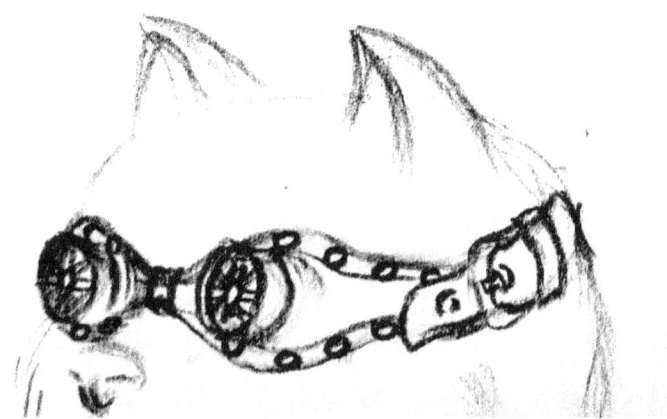

16. The smudges you see on the right of the closest frame suggests that the frame in embedded in the headband.

17. Draw inner lines on the right side of the headband.

18. Draw circles around the rim.

19. Draw curves and darken them in to make the middle of the goggles.

20. Draw circles around the left side as well.

21. Don't forget to draw curves to suggest the frame is embedded in the left part of the headband.

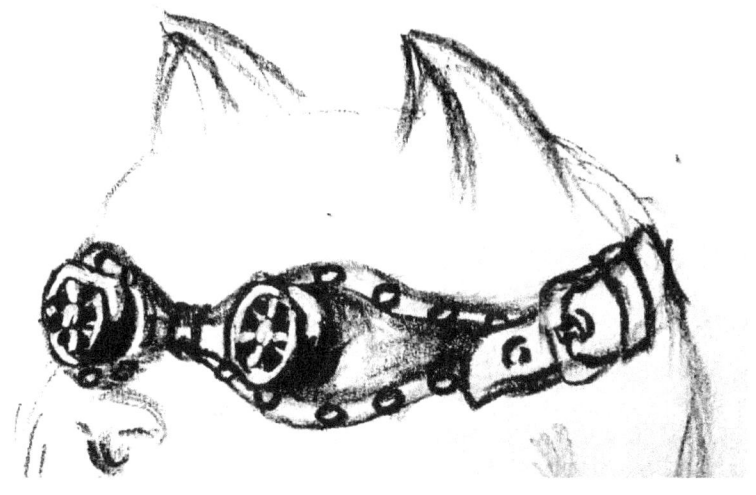

22. Shade in the part of the headband on the right side. Use a smudge stick to soften the shading.

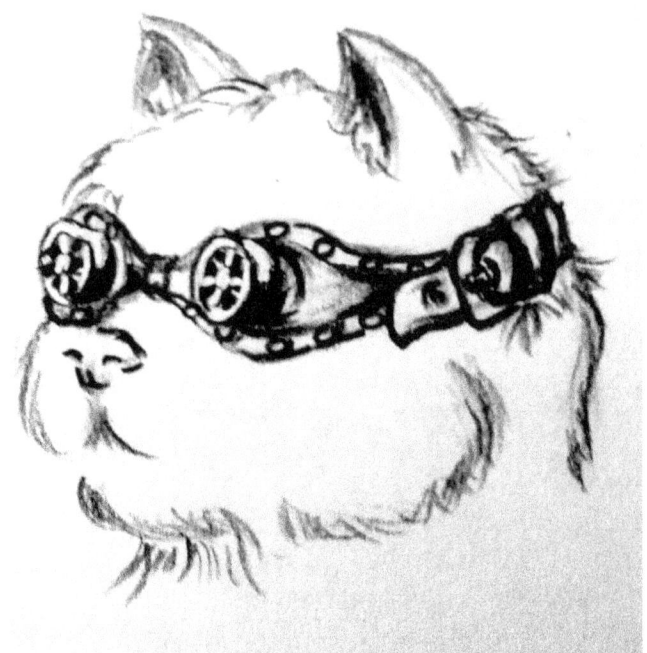

Take a soft lead and darken the fur, ears, and nose.

23. Add tufts of fur at the rear of the headband. This will make it more realistic.

24. Draw stray fur along the back of the head on top.

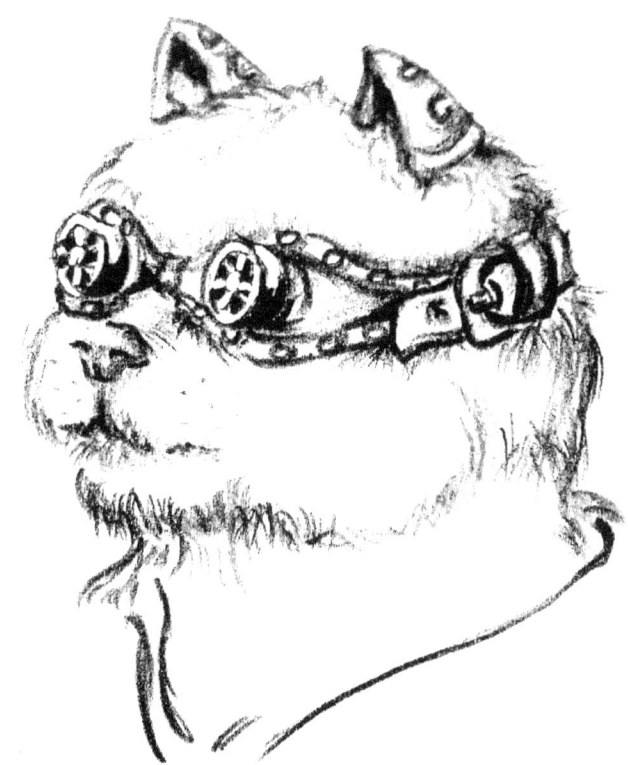

25. Here we have added a little bit of shading around the nose, goggles, and the back of the neck.

26. Draw curves for the collar.

27. Double up on the collar in the places you see in the picture.

28. Add the dots you see in the picture. We will be adding whiskers.

29. Finish out the mouth.

30. Add fur around the mouth.

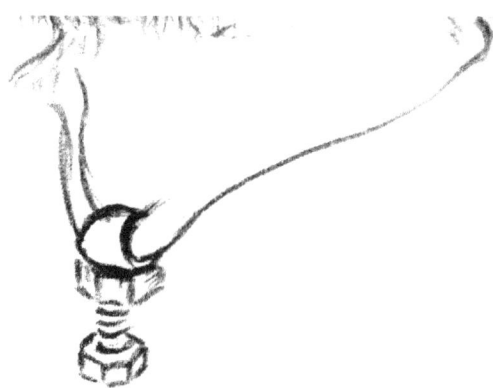

31. Draw curves for the pendant.

32. Darken the lines.

33. Draw a nut just below the bail.

34. Draw lines for the threads of the bolt.

35. Draw the head of the bolt.

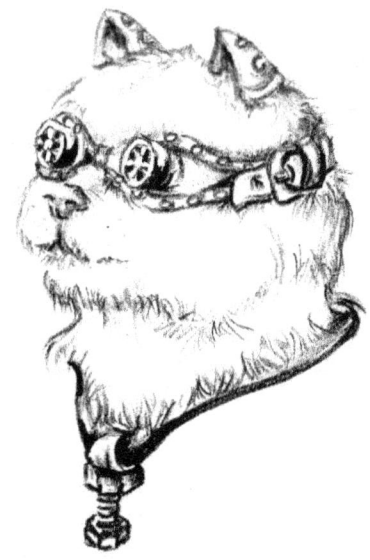

36. Darken the cord around the neck.

37. Shade in the bail, nut, threads and bolt.

38. Add fur around the collar.

39. Add a tuft of fur below the chin and jowl.

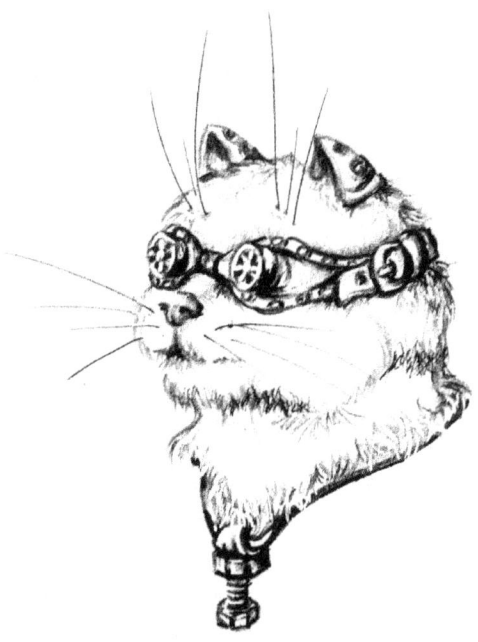

40. Add the whiskers you see in the picture.

41. Add the extra shading where you see it.

42. Add curves for the base of the ears.

43. Add circles for rivets.

44. Shade in the ears as you see in the picture.

Chapter 8 - About shading...

Shading can make or break a portrait, still life, and even landscape pictures. Take a look at the picture on the left. The light can make all the difference where the shadow falls. In this picture is the coming from the top right. There are a few things to notice:

1. Where the light hits the ball is white and without shading.

2. The shading on the ball grows darker the further it is from the light. This is due to the inability of the light to wrap around the object.

3. The shadow to the side of the ball gives the ball more of a 3-D quality.

4. The background shading allows us to focus on the ball.

5. The lighter shading under the ball to give us the feel of a surface under the ball. Proper shading lends depth to a picture. It also gives us more texture, and also the impression that the object in the picture is more than 2-D.

Practicing shading can be done by using an inanimate object and a light source you can move around. Take note as you draw. You will notice the closer the light is, the larger the shadow. The further the light source, the lesser the shadow becomes. You can you use the technique to practice shading faces by taking selfies at different angles to see how your face and features are shaded in the light.

Final Words

Like everything, it takes time and practice to perfect any hobby, and drawing Steampunk is no different. You can make it easier to practice by doing the following:

1. Collect and practice drawing cogs, gears, nuts, bolts, and other things hardware pieces that you can incorporate into your pieces.

2. Take note of the different types of metal plates that are used in this genre of art.

3. Take special notice of how fabric and leather drape on a person, chair, and other objects. Clothing, when drawn, shown give the illusion of movement. You can only do this by learning how it lays on people and different objects.

4. Look online for forums about Steampunk to inspiration and references to draw.

Always be on the look-out for new objects, and people you can draw in the genre. You can get all types of ideas from movies and books as well.

I hope this book has helped you get started on an exciting and imaginative genre. May you create beautiful scenes and objects.

www.ingramcontent.com/pod-product-compliance
Lightning Source LLC
Chambersburg PA
CBHW080611190526
45169CB00007B/2966